EXPERIENCES
AND
ENCOUNTERS

By

ZalZala

Noel Lorenz House of Fiction

www.noellorenz.com

Title of Book: *Experiences and Encounters*
Author of Book: Zal Zala

First Published in India in Dec 2021 Noel Lorenz House of Fiction

ISBN 13: 978-93-93695-20-8

Published and Printed By
Noel Lorenz House of Fiction
Headquarters - Kolkata, West Bengal, India
154A, KCG Road, Kolkata - 700050
www.noellorenz.com

ZalZala

Preface

Experiences and Encounters is a bouquet of English poems by ZalZala, a prominent poet from Mumbai, India.

\- Noel Lorenz

15 December 2021

Kolkata, India

Acknowledgements

It would be criminal if I do not thank so many people that are involved in the culmination of a book such as this.

First of all, I thank the team of NLHF for taking a decision to publish this book "Experiences and Encounters". This will be my first book of poetry in English and I express my gratitude towards them for taking a call to publish this.

English is a language of strategy and very different from the usual Urdu poetry that I write. The poems over here have been written taking into consideration this aspect of the English language. I would like to thank all my supporters globally and especially from Israel to have had this love for my short poems, which has inspired me to publish this book. Supporters like Oded Ievi, Lior Tourgeman, Mickey Wilf and so many of them have been the real reason for me to actually attempt to take out this book in English. I am sure I shall not disappoint them. I was also in a call with Steve McAffrey, our head of sales, where I introduced my hobbies as that of writing poems and he was looking forward to an English book. I believe, this has finally culminated into a reality.

ZalZala

I would like to thank the hous of "Hooted1ce" and its very humble proprietor Mr. Mohit Kumar, who has single handedly nurtured many budding talents in the field of poetry, music, comedy and various forms of performing arts in the busy city of Mumbai. Mohit, this really is a grand achievement that you need to be proud of.

Last but not the least, thank you so much my readers and poetry afficionados for showering you love towards me and encouraging me always to write new things.

ZalZala

Foreword

English poetry has always been a challenge for me. English is a language that I have used in my official communication, education, most of the communications that I do in a formal environment. Poetry in English has not been my forte. I learnt to write poems in Urdu and Bengali. However, having said that Imaginations do not have a language and it is due to this principle that I am daring to write many of my compositions in English. Many of these compositions that you see have been imagined in Urdu, but then have been formulated in English.

Being born and brought up in India, I have had this good opportunity to have had my brush with the English language as this language is a sort of inheritance we have had due to the history. Urdu is an invention of India but English is definitely an inheritance. It will be definitely interesting for you to read and go through the poems that have innovative imagination and inherited compositions.

Poetry is something that is not supposed to be read. A poet is not happy when his work is being read of appreciated. A poet is delighted when his words are imbibed, understood and then executed as soft principles in the society and life. A poet is less than a philosopher but certainly more than a writer. A poet is a deep thinker because he has to not only convey the message but has to convey it in a particular format with

ZalZala

brevity and alacrity. A poet's journey is continuous and incessant. A book of poems does not have one ending but several in form of several poems. A book of poetry conveys several thoughts in different sections and in different forms. A book of poetry is a reflection of someone's though process and probably is the best way to understand a person and most importantly life.

"Experiences and Encounters" these are the two words I choose to keep as a title of this book because most of the poems are corroborations of my experiences and encounters that I have had with life.

Therefore, happy reading….

Love

ZalZala

PS: I will use my Urdu Pen name, ZalZala, which means EarthQuake.

ZalZala

Contents

ZalZala

ZalZala

The Union

Was it like yesterday when we met or

Did time just take some twist and turns

Coz I am sure it ought to be like that

As in your sundering my whole life burns

I recall the peach of your cheek and sigh

The love that was, had reached so high

I think, I think and get forced to deduce

When thoughts that went stray would fuse

When you and me would be all but one

No troubles around no one to berate

Norms of the society and yes that hate

That hate that I saw in the eyes of your kin

That hate for me which made love a sin

Your sundering is not giving me the pain

Tis the hope that lingers around and hurts me

Tells me we will meet again

There will be a Union of thoughts, Coz after the heat

There will be rain

ZalZala

Ego

A macabre truth befalls me as I advance in
encomium

I see a demon, devouring you my love and malice
all around

Malaised and razed I look around and try to
triangulate

The nemesis that tries to mar us, I try to locate

But I fail to find that wretched demon as

It resides in you somehow

Its called the ego, your evil self

That makes your rectitude take a bow

My love was pure, unabashed I was

When the two eyes of ours met

Little I knew this journey present

Would make your visions go wet

ZalZala

You could have for once allowed your anger to
subside

You could have for once allowed Logic by your side

Little would we have a chance so that love departs

Your Ego, yes your ego made the blossoming love

Ripped in pieces and parts

ZalZala

Water and Love

Yes, it was your choice, colorless and odorless

Just like water, which is all around everywhere

Blends with everything and every occasion

Yet seems that it's there, Nowhere

Need to just accept, It is there…

That is what you wanted alone, to imbibe

That is what you wanted alone, to ablude

So simple and pure, just like your love

So touching the heart and never rude

Your love, was that water, that flowed all along

Like a river, serene and ready to pacify

You were the solvent that were always there

Incessant, abundant… ready to purify

ZalZala

I envy my luck as I be on your side

Just looking at you like a parched terrain

And I be enthralled and anxiously wait

Wait for yours to come like a rain

ZalZala

What Am I?

I am that piece of exclusivity

That cannot be fathomed in your dream

Know me not as the settled sugar

In a cappuccino I am the cream

Surely it takes time to know me

Surely I am vast

So take your time, slow and steady

Let your thoughts not run fast.

Coz I am not the car in a dump yard

I am that Rolles Royce, an expensive dream

Not so free, and definitely not fair

Even dreaming me attracts a fare

I surely am an expensive dream

In the Cappuccino I am the cream

ZalZala

Blooming like a Lily

The moonlit night caresses your slender body

And there is me, the happy soul, which

Just wanders within the realms of your silhouette

Vanquished by your charms and love

Don't take me away from this world little

I am happy just happy to be in your cove

Let me be like the Pupa, enslaved in the hard bounds

Of your passion ignited, your love so soft

Let me not be free again, let me be the

Barn in your lovely croft.

I am happy to see you in a state like this

Satiated and wet, craving for more

Dry vocals let out some sweet moan

The moments of passion causing furore.

ZalZala

The sweet and sour moments that we made love

The moments that abashed the moon

The moments that are now memoires in the page of time

The memoires that will fade away soon

The night of the passion moon souls ignited

Kills the flavors in time that were of gloom

And when it's the morn after a passionate night

Like a fresh Lily my dear you bloom

ZalZala

That was all!!!

So, you still remember the time of joy

You still know how we just went ahead

With every thing that the world despised

Our love just kept them surprised

With the fact that it was ahead of time

I dared to love you, you cared for me

When a love of that kind, you and me

From worlds afar, was seen as criminal

Me going to rever the Idol and you the infinity

Impossible was the name of possibility

However, we dared, we dared to look

From an angle that would be acute

With us both only in the grabs of its arms

And our love surrounded all of us

And that was all

That was all that we needed to make things move

In a sticky marshy land make us groove

ZalZala

In the music that was mellowed to melody

That was all we needed

Thirst

Those rosy lips that were dripping

The inviting droplets of prurience

Attracted I was surely with their brilliance

They were like the sparse source

To quench my thirsty soul

They were like the reigns of my thoughts

Keeping me in control

I just wanted to drown myself

In the purity of their carnal thoughts

I just wanted to be candidate, who

Shows the way how it is done

So that you are now pinned to me and to none

This thirst, I tell you is a constant thing

That just comes on and on, and I am dry

I am dry always, seeking your lips.

I know not how to keep steady

How much ever I try

ZalZala

What are you to me

First there were the times

When time stood still

Your presence, yes it was,

There present to kill

To kill time for me so that

I am engrossed in your aura that spread

Like the wildfire spreads in a forest

But then there is that gust of wind

Your absence that is, which makes

Most of the fatigue put to rest...

Talking bout fatigue lemme remind

You have been stressful and not so kind

You are my fatigue and you are my strain

But your absence is my biggest pain

You are my evenings sorted with wine

You are my mornings with crispy sunshine

ZalZala

You are my energy and you are my time

A second without you, is a crime

Droplets of dew on a fine autumn morn

On the lilies out in my garden

And within my heart torn

ZalZala

Alone under the crescent moon

The crescent moon pierces me with your memories

The nights when tides of sea were comrades of love

Tonight it just hangs alone in the sky

Like a desperate and injured dove

The silent breeze that once accessed your cheeks

Today is no less than a dagger

Without you by my side

Even a stable life makes me stagger

The rains just be my companion

To hide my eyes full of tears

The clouds act as a mighty qwilt

To shun away my fears

Coz I am alone with all myself

I cannot escape the fall

ZalZala

If you were there to hold my hand

I would not have broken at all....

ZalZala

I salute your Folly

Was I a fool to love you

Or it was the other way

I salute your folly my dear

To not love me and turn away

Your choice of partner is as clear

As the choice of okra by a house wife

She tosses and turns the poor dead thing

And this way just wastes away her life

You are a hopeless case of fruitless ambition

You are like a shadow in a dark room

I guess you were not looking around for love

You were searching for a milking groom

Tall, Handsome and a fat paycheck

Were the things for which you cared

ZalZala

True love!!! Well trash it away
The concept just got you scared

Just like a wild bird that you were like
I released you from my love slowly
Then I saw you fade out in the polluted sky
And thereafter, as I say, I saluted your folly

ZalZala

The letters I did not post

Those were some words emancipated

They just came out of my pen and

Well, my love for you still stays corroborated

Locked in some pages are my feelings that haven't
travelled the distance.

The distance between our hearts and minds

For sure I am yet to cross that imaginary fence

Which borders your essence from me

And that is why these pieces of paper

Ornate with my feelings in ink...

Just stay.... They just stay.... Free with me...

ZalZala

You might not remember

I sent you the last flower before the fall
I plucked it from the Eden before it withered
Yes, the lord knows well, I did it all
Kindled the Fire when it was all simmered

You many not remember the errands I made
You may not remember the words I said
However, I am still in awe of your grace
The grace that bent the time and space.

Yes, today they call it gravity for sure
But then for me twas a magic
And the time, a magical phase.

ZalZala

The Autumn Delight

Oh there she stands in her white gown

She is Autumn, bidding goodbye to the rain

She is the new lady in the town

With her soft due drops to caress the terain

There she is blooming with flowers at night

Creations momentary that fall in the day

Over the dew drenched meadows

The pain of rain they take away

Floating white clouds make shapes in sky

Some heart, some demons off they fly

They are the last marching soldiers of rain

They are the monsoons effort vain

Still they are so ornate around

Kissing goodbye to the grateful ground

Autumn morning and nights are here

ZalZala

The rains are retreating, and giving a salute

A promise from them to come next year.

ZalZala

Taking things slow

There is a whole full night to go
Can't be in a hurry for times at stake
I can't hasten my love for you
So please, please, let's take it slow

Tis the slow simmering flame
Which brews taste into a meal
Tis the slow intake of breath
That infuses life with zeal

Slowly passing moments of the night
Makes the petals of the Lilly glow
That's why... That is why.... I say
I like to take things a bit slow

ZalZala

I saw two moons today

It was the same night sky, dark and stary

And there it was, draped in a shiny white gown

Arising from the eastern end of the endless sky

Throwing its shimmer flamboyantly down

But then lo!!! What was that new light

Which rivalled those dropping from the heavens.

The rays were pure and proximal to me

Shot like arrows towards me raging a fight

For sure they were not those coming from above

They were lethal and then they were sooting

They charmed more than they lit

On a night like this, when the heartbeats soar

They seemed to be deemed fit

So!!! Is it a miracle today?

Coz I do not fathom why this boon is showered
today

I see the moon embracing me with her hands

And the other moon, up above, shying away

ZalZala

Do not think it happens often

I think it is my lucky day

Coz the full blue moon has lit up my sky

And you have shone all the way

I see the God's pinch themselves for this

Coz I saw two moons today

I saw two moons today.

ZalZala

I could not afford

I could bear all the malaise that's there around
Could not afford the distance between you and me...
I was able to jump the highest walls in this world
Could not afford the fence between you and me

There is abyss that I have been to often
Could not afford the crevice between you and me
Have seen the game of avarice shaping across me
However, could not afford the malice between you
and me

Losing the world was an expense that I not fear
But losing you alone was a cost so dear
Coz you, my love, were the world I knew
I could drain an ocean for a drop of your dew

ZalZala

Love... An Apocalypse

If there be an apocalypse

Let that begin with your smile

So that in awe of disaster

I live along for a while

The torsion in the heart

Tumult that grows in mind is

Like the layers of onions

Let this life unwind

The life that is multifacet

Still enslaved in your dream

The heart that beats relentlessly

Lending out a silent scream

Coz love is no less than an apocalypse

Tis balance of hope and despair

ZalZala

There are victors and there are the vanquished

In this battle that's so unfair

ZalZala

Do not wait on the balcony

I am no more the Romeo of your life my dear

Do not wait for me on the Balcony

I am a warrior that is long gone on field

Over the times have become ruthless indeed

With the battles around me love has bled

Emotions and encomiums from my heart has fled

Dexterity has taken the place of romance

And life… yes life… is just a mere trance

So let me go and deal with all of this

You stay away from this pathetic cacophony

Do not wait for me on the Balcony.

The roses that I wanted to give you

Have suddenly withered in cruel times

The deafening noise of the opiated world

Have lulled the sounds of the wind-chimes

But then I can still hear your laughter

ZalZala

It may be slow, it may be mild

It is the only reason to live here

In a world so adult, I feel like a child.

However, this dream may not last for long

Coz there are raiders of happiness here

Who are hell bent to break a symphony

That's why I say aloud, and without a doubt

Do not wait for me on the Balcony

ZalZala

Your love is contagious

Your Love, my dear, is a contagious disease

Passes from me to all whom I meet

So strange is your city my darling

Every single heart just falls on your feet

Tried I to save thyself from this catastrophe

But then the lightning had to strike once

I had to be enslaved in this bonding

I had to finally fall in a trance

But then was it me alone who was the prey

I saw all around people swept away

They were all falling for you like house of cards

As and when they saw your hair sway

I wonder if I could be vaccinated

To save myself from this love devastating

But then I wonder what a vaccine is

Tis the same germ minus gestating

ZalZala

A dormant form of your love that is

That would make me sort of Immune

Would that be an interesting stuff

Or would it be a song off-tune?

Happy I am to be sick in your love

Contagious it might be. So what?

Let this feeling be a pandemic of sorts…

Dangerous it might be. So what?

ZalZala

You are guilty of igniting

This fire that burns my heart all day long

I did not bring it with me along

Was it only my fault to fall in love with you

Was it only me who sang the love song

Coz when with my body my soul burns along

The flame of love just came out shining

And it's just not me who is guilty of this

You too are guilty of igniting

May these shadow of clouds

Not be just for the sake of it

May they also shower the raindrops cold

So that it can quench the thirst, long born

I have waited for long, in solitude

To tell you my feelings long untold

Tired am I, with me long fighting

Tis not only me who is at fault here

You too are guilty of igniting

ZalZala

Guilty you are of igniting the passion

That flows today like a lava in me

ZalZala

The barbed wire

The barbed wire of mistrust

Love with its thorny patches

Some hope of proximity and

Page of life with scratches

Do I still see the good times?

Or have they withered away?

Is there a moment of joy here?

Or the pain is here to stay?

ZalZala

That forbidden love

Twas that story of forbidden love

That always rings around my ears

Coz whenever I dare to Love her

I am cornered by my fears.

The fear of losing her from my life

The fear of she being like a lightening

That shines in the night sky for a while

But then just dissolves in time with a smile.

I fear the pain that I bear for her

Lest my tolerance just gives way.

Tis a torture that goes on and on.

Tis a matter, that I cannot say.

ZalZala

You Errupt... I Explode

As your taste lingers on my lips

I feel a sense of wild black berries.

Intoxicating and yet sweet and sticky

Like a bee that hops over tulips.

Bedroom filled with deafening moan

Scratches on my body, now not alone.

The tangy taste of your lusty flesh

Stays around my mind afresh.

Your navel, a hot thirsty crater

Your feminism errupts like a volcano

And the sheets go wet with ecstatic water.

My senses now not in my reigns

As they are now knocked out of my brains.

I knew I was in the heaven abode.

But then your love just made me explode.

ZalZala

Just for you

This blooming rose that you see

Has been crimsoned by the blood I give.

I have bloomed gardens of Eden like this

Because for you my love I die, I live.

There were instances of pained existence

And there was my rendering love for you

There were embers of the heated passion

And some portions of endearing love for you.

My breath and my heartbeats do sync not

And without you around, I stay disarrayed

Rhymes and rhythms dance often with me

But without you around, they remain stayed.

So these thoughts and words are just for you

So these emotions like swords just for you.

Tons of Love with eons to spare

Tis just for you that I care.

ZalZala

I have fled

I have left alone to saline streams that exited my
eyes in some lonely unknown place.

Coz these days I am busy in my life that is going
along in its pace.

Love that was has just left an ember.

And you my dear, I don't remember.

I don't remember the strikes that you made

On my weak heart that day and night bled.

I don't remember the tortures anymore

For I am done with all this, I have fled.

Fled I have to the land's end and where

There would be just my thoughts and me.

Fled I have like a coward if you would say

For I am just now what I want to be.

ZalZala

Living on

A dream that lingers on still on my eyes with all its might

Tis a vision for which i do not mind to give a fight.

So what if the world just did not want to approve

So what if there were more thorns than flowers on the plate

I need to just hang on with my life and sit tight

Coz this tussle between my heart and my mind is freaking me out

If you just be by my side and hold my hand

I can go on and on with this fight.

While there are options of going to sleep for me

While there are options of just pulling the plug.

What I want is just to be a little bit intrepid here.

What I want is still to play the war of tug.

Coz this war is not for you or me alone.

ZalZala

I know death will get the better of me,

Till then

Just living on

ZalZala

Reminisces

As the sun bids adieu in the western sky
And finally takes a vermillion bow.
I take my load and turn back home
Make my path with a pace too slow.

The shedding trees of the autumn winds
Pity on my state today.
As a lonesome lover I trek along
With a long face and dismay.

Strictly speaking those days that were
Annuls of alleged bliss
As I see them through the looking glass
Just want to give them a royal miss.

An axe it was, the thing called love
Cuts me well, but not uproots.

ZalZala

Injured me and I had bled,

It pleases me well when it suits

I had bid adieu to all my feels

They caused me a lot of pain.

As I see the days in retrospect

Don't want to fall in love again.

ZalZala

Façade

Happiness on the facade

Restlessness in mind.

Under her breezy eyes

A deluge I find!

A deluge I find!

Raking pains of the past

Her future is embalmed.

I look beyond her beauty

I look beyond her looks

And then I get calmed.

And then I get calmed.

ZalZala

About the Book

As the life goes on unidirectionally with its ups and downs, two very important things alter its course time and again.

Experiences: Corroborations of the events that have happened.

Encounters: A livid description of incidents more impromptu and antithetical at times from experiences.

"Love", being a common factor of both is expressed through these two aspects.

ZalZala

About ZalZala

A telecommunications professional working in the wild regions of Africa and helping that continent continuously to develop the infrastructure of communications and next generation services, Kalyan,

also writes poetries by the pen name of ZalZala. He insists that he wants to be known by the name of ZalZala in the poetry circle so we would address him by that name. ZalZala is an Urdu word and it means "Earthquake". The style of writing of ZalZala is no less than an earthquake as it turns many people's thinking topsy turvy. ZalZala has a knack to look at things in a totally different way than it is actually perceived and that makes him totally different from all other poets. His distinctively different attitude towards Urdu poetry is something that needs to be watched out for always and that is why he is special. In this section he has written poems and cared to explain the gist or provide translation wherever it is possible. ZalZala also believes that Urdu is one of India's amazing creation as a language and a very precious gift

ZalZala

that India had to give its Child nation after the partition. ZalZala believes that Urdu is the most modern language with an exquisite detail towards the phonetics.

In this collection, ZalZala has written poems on love and emotions related to it. Of course there are different forms of love that are addressed over here and it is not limited only to the "Love" we interpret.

ZalZala loves to connect with new people always and you can get in touch with ZalZala on Instagram @zalzala_kalyan

ZalZala

~End~

ZalZala

www.noellorenz.com

ZalZala